ONE CHAPTER A DAY

GoodMorningGirls.org

The Book of Judges

© 2016 Women Living Well Ministries, LLC

ALL RIGHTS RESERVED

No part of this book may be reproduced in any form or by any electronic or mechanical means, including information storage and retrieval systems, without written permission from the author, except in the case of a reviewer, who may quote brief passages embodied in critical articles or in a review.

Scripture is from the ESV® Bible (The Holy Bible, English Standard Version®), copyright © 2001 by Crossway Bibles, a publishing ministry of Good News Publishers. Used by permission. All rights reserved.

Welcome to Good Morning Girls! We are so glad you are joining us.

God created us to walk with Him, to know Him, and to be loved by Him. He is our living well, and when we drink from the water He continually provides, His living water will change the entire course of our lives.

> *Jesus said: "Whoever drinks of the water that I will give him will never be thirsty again. The water that I will give him will become in him a spring of water welling up to eternal life." ~ John 4:14 (ESV)*

So let's begin.

The method we use here at GMG is called the **SOAK** method.

- ❒ **S**—The S stands for *Scripture*—Read the chapter for the day. Then choose 1-2 verses and write them out word for word. (There is no right or wrong choice—just let the Holy Spirit guide you.)

- ❒ **O**—The O stands for *Observation*—Look at the verse or verses you wrote out. Write 1 or 2 observations. What stands out to you? What do you learn about the character of God from these verses? Is there a promise, command or teaching?

- ❒ **A**—The A stands for *Application*—Personalize the verses. What is God saying to you? How can you apply them to your life? Are there any changes you need to make or an action to take?

- ❒ **K**—The K stands for *Kneeling in Prayer*—Pause, kneel and pray. Confess any sin God has revealed to you today. Praise God for His word. Pray the passage over your own life or someone you love. Ask God to help you live out your applications.

SOAK God's word into your heart and squeeze every bit of nourishment you can out of each day's scripture reading. Soon you will find your life transformed by the renewing of your mind!

Walk with the King!

Courtney

WomenLivingWell.org, GoodMorningGirls.org

Join the GMG Community

Share your daily SOAK at 7:45am on **Facebook.com/GoodMorningGirlsWLW**

Instagram: WomenLivingWell #GoodMorningGirls

GMG Bible Coloring Chart

COLORS	KEYWORDS
PURPLE	God, Jesus, Holy Spirit, Saviour, Messiah
PINK	women of the Bible, family, marriage, parenting, friendship, relationships
RED	love, kindness, mercy, compassion, peace, grace
GREEN	faith, obedience, growth, fruit, salvation, fellowship, repentance
YELLOW	worship, prayer, praise, doctrine, angels, miracles, power of God, blessings
BLUE	wisdom, teaching, instruction, commands
ORANGE	prophecy, history, times, places, kings, genealogies, people, numbers, covenants, vows, visions, oaths, future
BROWN/GRAY	Satan, sin, death, hell, evil, idols, false teachers, hypocrisy, temptation

Introduction to the Book of Judges

"In those days, there was no king in Israel. Everyone did what was right in his own eyes." Judges 17:6

Judges is a book about 12 judges who helped deliver the nation of Israel from one of the darkest and most oppressed times in their history. These judges were far from perfect but God used them in mighty ways.

As Joshua ends, we see the nation taking a stand for God. As we enter Judges; however, we see that the claim that Joshua made at the end of his book has come true. The people are following after other gods and there is a rapid decline - both as a nation and individually. The book of Judges focuses on sin and consequences. Sin grows when it is left unattended.

This book sounds a lot like today. Many choose to do what is right in their own eyes and follow after the ways of the world. But we can be like the 12 judges - who, though they were flawed and imperfect, decided to depend on God and be obedient to Him. Most of all, we can see that just like the judges - God's mercy has come to our rescue over and over again.

Key Verse: *"In those days, there was no king in Israel. Everyone did what was right in his own eyes."* Judges 17:6

The Outline:

1. **The failure of Israel (Judges 1:1-3:6)**
   The nation of Israel had compromised God's commands to drive out the inhabitants of the land.

2. **The Judges (3:7-16:31)**
   We see the nation of Israel sinning over and over again because of the compromise that they had made. Sin always has consequences.

3. **The Moral Failure of Israel (17:1-21:25)**
   Despite the efforts of Israel's judges, the people would not turn their whole hearts back to God. They did what was right in their own eyes. The result was a decline of the nation - spiritually, morally, and politically.

Themes:

Compromise: Whenever a judge died, the people faced a decline and they compromised their standards. Society has rewarded compromise. We need to not compromise what we know is right from the standard of God's Word.

Apostasy: We can expect decay when we value anything more highly than God. In Judges, idol worship and man-made religion led to a complete abandoning of their walk with God. We can have idols and man-made religion as well today by focusing on anything more than we do on our relationship with God.

Repentance: The decline, decay and defeat of the nation of Israel caused them to call out to God for help. When they repented, God delivered them. Idolatry gains a stronghold in our hearts and lives when we place anything above God. We need to watch for modern idolatry in our hearts and minds.

I'm so excited to begin the book of Judges with you. This is not going to be an easy read. Parts of this book are very dark. The people of Israel repeatedly fell into a cycle of doing what was right in their own eyes, then calling out to God for help, then God raised up judges to deliver them, but then they would go astray once again. There is violence and sin and disobedience scattered throughout this book but there is also grace and mercy and the mighty hand of God's deliverance, laid out for us all to see. Let's get started.

Keep walking with the King!

Special Thanks

I want to extend a special thank you to Mandy Kelly, Rosilind Jukic, Bridget Childress and Misty Leask for your help with this journal. Your love, dedication and leadership to the Good Morning Girls ministry is such a blessing to all. Thank you for giving to the Lord.

~ Courtney

The Lord said,

"Judah shall go up; behold,

I have given the land into his hand."

Judges 1:2

Reflection Question:

Manasseh, Ephraim, Zebulan, Asher and Naphtali failed to drive the inhabitants off their land as they were commanded.

Name a time when you only partially did what God laid on your heart. How did that situation turn out?

Judges 1

S—The S stands for ***Scripture***

O—The O stands for ***Observation***

A—The A stands for ***Application***

K—The K stands for ***Kneeling in Prayer***

And there arose another generation after them who did not know the Lord or the work that he had done for Israel.

Judges 2:10

Reflection Question:

Israel turned their backs on God and began to seek out new gods.

Is there something in your own life that you seem to seek out more than God?

Judges 2

S—The S stands for *Scripture*

O—The O stands for *Observation*

A—The A stands for *Application*

K—The K stands for *Kneeling in Prayer*

And the people of Israel did what was evil in the sight of the Lord.

Judges 3:7

Reflection Question:

Israel was tested to see if they would obey God's commandments. Each time they failed the test.

Have you been tested in your Christian walk lately? In what ways?

Judges 3

S—The S stands for **Scripture**

O—The O stands for **Observation**

A—The A stands for **Application**

K—The K stands for **Kneeling in Prayer**

And Deborah said to Barak, "Up! For this is the day in which the Lord has given Sisera into your hand. Does not the Lord go out before you?"

Judges 4:14

Reflection Question:

Barak didn't want to move forward with the plan God had already laid out for him without Deborah.

Name a time when you have been too afraid or unwilling to do what God has asked of you because you didn't want to do it alone?

Judges 4

S—The S stands for **Scripture**

O—The O stands for **Observation**

A—The A stands for **Application**

K—The K stands for **Kneeling in Prayer**

So may all your enemies perish, O Lord!

But your friends be like the sun

as he rises in his might.

Judges 5:31

Reflection Question:

Deborah and Barak's song tells us, the people offered themselves willingly.

Do you offer yourself up willingly for God or do you struggle with giving over complete control?

Judges 5

S—The S stands for **Scripture**

O—The O stands for **Observation**

A—The A stands for **Application**

K—The K stands for **Kneeling in Prayer**

Peace be to you.

Do not fear.

Judges 6:23

Reflection Question:

Gideon asked God to show him a sign that God was truly wanting him to go into battle for His people.

Name a time, when you have questioned God. What was His response to you?

Judges 6

S—The S stands for **Scripture**

O—The O stands for **Observation**

A—The A stands for **Application**

K—The K stands for **Kneeling in Prayer**

As soon as Gideon heard the telling of the dream and its interpretation, he worshiped.

Judges 7:15

Reflection Question:

God can make great things happen even out of the smallest of things. He does this to remind us that He is with us.

How does this bring encouragement to you today with the situations you are facing?

Judges 7

S—The S stands for **Scripture**

O—The O stands for **Observation**

A—The A stands for **Application**

K—The K stands for **Kneeling in Prayer**

Gideon said to them,

"I will not rule over you,

and my son will not rule over you;

the Lord will rule over you."

Judges 8:23

Reflection Question:

Even after all God had done, the people still longed for a leader. Gideon refused; reminding them that God alone was their ruler.

In what ways do you find it hard to let God be the ruler of your life?

Judges 8

S—The S stands for **Scripture**

O—The O stands for **Observation**

A—The A stands for **Application**

K—The K stands for **Kneeling in Prayer**

Come and reign over us.

Judges 9:10

Reflection Question:

Abimelech rose up over God's people using power and influence. Yet, in the end, God caused him to fail.

This reminds us that God is always in control. How does this bring you comfort today?

Judges 9

S—The S stands for **Scripture**

O—The O stands for **Observation**

A—The A stands for **Application**

K—The K stands for **Kneeling in Prayer**

The people of Israel cried out to the Lord, saying, "We have sinned against you, because we have forsaken our God and have served the Baals."

Judges 10:10

Reflection Question:

Once again, Israel was overtaken because they had turned their backs on God and instead chose to worship false gods.

Has God ever revealed to you, that you were placing other gods before Him?

Judges 10

S—The S stands for **Scripture**

O—The O stands for **Observation**

A—The A stands for **Application**

K—The K stands for **Kneeling in Prayer**

All that the Lord our God has given us, we will possess.

Judges 11:24

Reflection Question:

Jephthah remained confident in God's promises knowing that God would prevail.

Name a time when you faced a situation when you had to remind yourself that God's promises would be fulfilled no matter what.

Judges 11

S—The S stands for **Scripture**

O—The O stands for **Observation**

A—The A stands for **Application**

K—The K stands for **Kneeling in Prayer**

The Lord gave them into my hand.

Judges 12:3

Reflection Question:

God and God alone can save us, not man.

Name a time that God has stepped in and rescued you from a horrible situation.

Judges 12

S—The S stands for **Scripture**

O—The O stands for **Observation**

A—The A stands for **Application**

K—The K stands for **Kneeling in Prayer**

*And the woman bore a son
and called his name Samson.
And the young man grew,
and the Lord blessed him.*

Judges 13:24

Reflection Question:

Monoah sought out God's instructions. God was faithful in revealing their duties.

When was the last time you sought direction from God?

Judges 13

S—The S stands for *Scripture*

O—The O stands for *Observation*

A—The A stands for *Application*

K—The K stands for *Kneeling in Prayer*

Then the Spirit of the Lord rushed upon him.

Judges 14:6

Reflection Question:

The Spirit of the Lord came upon Samson twice in this chapter. This shows the involvement of God in Samson's life.

How have you seen God's involvement in your life?

Judges 14

S—The S stands for **Scripture**

O—The O stands for **Observation**

A—The A stands for **Application**

K—The K stands for **Kneeling in Prayer**

And he called upon the Lord and said, "You have granted this great salvation by the hand of your servant."

Judges 15:18

Reflection Question:

Even though Samson was strong, he knew he had to call on God to help him.

Have you ever been in a situation where you were determined to fix the situation yourself, only to be reminded by God, that you must rely on Him and not yourself?

Judges 15

S—The S stands for **Scripture**

O—The O stands for **Observation**

A—The A stands for **Application**

K—The K stands for **Kneeling in Prayer**

O Lord God,

please remember me

and please strengthen me.

Judges 16:28

Reflection Question:

Samson's choice to follow his own human nature allowed him to be captured by his enemies.

Name a time when you ignored God's instructions and you failed.

Judges 16

S—The S stands for **Scripture**

O—The O stands for **Observation**

A—The A stands for **Application**

K—The K stands for **Kneeling in Prayer**

In those days there was no king in Israel. Everyone did what was right in his own eyes.

Judges 17:6

Reflection Question:

During these times, everyone did what was right in their own eyes.

What problems arise when we all do what we feel is right instead of seeking out God's counsel first?

Judges 17

S—The S stands for **Scripture**

O—The O stands for **Observation**

A—The A stands for **Application**

K—The K stands for **Kneeling in Prayer**

Go in peace.

The journey on which you go

is under the eye of the Lord.

Judges 18:6

Reflection Question:

The priest was easily convinced to help those who robbed Micah with the promise of a promotion.

Have you ever been placed in a situation where you had to choose between personal desires and God's desires?

Judges 18

S—The S stands for **Scripture**

O—The O stands for **Observation**

A—The A stands for **Application**

K—The K stands for **Kneeling in Prayer**

Peace be to you.

Judges 19:20

Reflection Question:

The Levite and the man of the house protected themselves over the protection of the women in the home. They selfishly did what was right in their own eyes.

Selfishness hurts those around us, especially those in our own home. Do you struggle with selfishness in your home?

Judges 19

S—The S stands for **Scripture**

O—The O stands for **Observation**

A—The A stands for **Application**

K—The K stands for **Kneeling in Prayer**

Purge evil.

Judges 20:13

Reflection Question:

God waited until Israel was willing to confront their own sin before delivering the victory to them against the tribe of Benjamin.

Is there something God is attempting to get you to confront, so that He can bless you?

Judges 20

S—The S stands for **Scripture**

O—The O stands for **Observation**

A—The A stands for **Application**

K—The K stands for **Kneeling in Prayer**

In those days

there was no king in Israel.

Everyone did what was right

in his own eyes.

Judges 21:25

Reflection Question:

The tribe of Benjamin was allowed to rebuild after they had been dealt with.

Name a time that you had to rebuild certain areas of your own life to get back on track with God.

Judges 21

S—The S stands for **Scripture**

O—The O stands for **Observation**

A—The A stands for **Application**

K—The K stands for **Kneeling in Prayer**

Made in the USA
Middletown, DE
25 April 2021